Saltwater
FLY FISHING
MAGIC

PIERRE AFFRE

By Neal and Linda Rogers
with Lefty Kreh and Stu Apte

Illustrations by Craig Rogers • Design and Layout by Len Eckel

Contributing Photographers:

Pierre Affre • George Anderson • Karl "Andy" Anderson • Stu Apte
Joel Arrington • R. Valentine Atkinson • José Azel • Bill Barnes • Dan Blanton
Jeffrey Cardenas • Hanson Carroll • Trey Combs • Nick Curcione
Gil Drake • Chico Fernandez • Christine Fong • Rod Harrison
Ed Jaworowski • Lefty Kreh • Bob McNally • Brian O'Keefe • Timothy O'Keefe
Tony Oswald • C. Boyd Pfeiffer • Joe Richard • Craig Rogers • Linda Rogers
Neal Rogers • Jack Samson • Dale Spartas • Bob Stearns • Walt Stearns
David Stoecklein • Sam Talarico • Bobbi Wolverton • Mike Wolverton

Distributed by LYONS & BURFORD

SPECIAL THANKS
to our friends and teachers

Kathleen and Juergen Kreuger
EL PESCADOR
Chet Pryor and Bob Berger
H. T. CHITTUM
Tom Richardson, Barry Gibson
and Spider Andresen
SALT WATER SPORTSMAN
Bob LeFever
FRAN JOHNSON'S
George Hommel
WORLDWIDE SPORTSMAN
Howard Obenhoff
Mary Comba
Mariann Matosich
Carlos Marin
George Radel
Capt. Bill Smith
Pedro Cano Canseco
Brendan Burke
Kelly Wade
Nick Lyons
Vic Dunaway
Billy Rabito
Russell Chatham
&
Mark Thompson

Published in 1993 by Earth and Great
Weather Publishing Company
202 South Montana Street
Butte, Montana 59701
Phone: 406-723-6526
FAX: 406-782-3712

Distributed by
Lyons & Burford
31 West 21st Street
New York, New York 10010

Design and Layout by
Len Eckel
Len Visual Design
40 South Last Chance Gulch
Helena, Montana 59601

ISBN 1-55821-253-1

Printed in Hong Kong

**Dedicated to our fathers
Martin Rigrotsky and Curtis Howard
*They always had time to take us fishing***

MARATHON, FLORIDA

4

Introduction

A tropical morning calm with promise. It's a Tarpon Day! Tall, billowing clouds tower above a glassy flat. Songs of shore birds fade into the distance as a guide poles quietly into the brightening sky. The sun peeks above the rim of the earth, transforming muted colors to gold. Suddenly the tarpon are there, rolling peacefully and methodically in the distance. They turn, and the procession aims itself toward the angler on the bow. Trembling with excitement he readies— fly line, reel, and rod. The tarpon come into range 80 feet away. Small wavelets glisten off their backs as they continue rolling. Time stops as the cast is made. The orange and yellow fly drops in front of the lead fish. A sudden rush and he has it, turning away, making a gaping slash in the once quiet water. Set the hook—clear the line—bow to the first mighty jump—hold on—rod high. This magnificent game continues on in the most beautiful setting anyone could wish to see.

This is what this book is about. The magic game of fly fishing in saltwater is as beautiful as it is exciting. Our photographers have taken time away from fishing to record these special moments for all of us to see. We hope that their efforts will make you feel like you're there with them, freezing a spectacular instant into a photograph for all to share.

Come join us.

Feel the Magic!

Neal Rogers
&
Linda Rogers
1993

5

CRAIG ROGERS PHOTO

INTRODUCTION

By Lefty Kreh

STU APTE

F ly fishing has been a vital part of my life for nearly fifty years. Aside from my family, it has been my greatest source of pleasure, and luck has allowed me to make fly fishing my primary source of income for decades.

I can recall, as if it had happened yesterday, my first significant experience with fly fishing. In 1945 I returned home to Maryland from the battle front of World War II. During the next two years I managed to fish most of the spring, summer, and fall, mainly for my favorite fresh water fish, the smallmouth bass. I often used bait but enjoyed trying to catch bass with artificial lures a great deal more. Spinning was in its infancy and most of my fishing was with what was considered state-of-the-art tackle at that time--tiny, narrow-spool tournament casting reels, filled with braided nylon line. The rods were made from a new material developed during the war– "fiberglass."

Quickly, I established a local reputation as a hot-shot bass fisherman, and local newspapers wrote stories about my catches. Like many young people who don't realize how little they really know, I thought I was something special.

Then, I met Joe Brooks. Joe, already a fairly well-known fly fisherman/outdoor writer, lived near me. Hearing of my ability to catch smallmouth bass, Joe asked me to take him fishing. The next morning I carried a laminated wood canoe down the bank of the Potomac River near Harper's Ferry. I looked at Joe and was amazed to see that he was rigging a fly rod. It was a summer day and there was a warm brisk breeze blowing. I humbly suggested to Joe that it didn't look like a very good day for fly fishing and he might like to use one of my plug-casting outfits. Always a perfect gentleman, Joe quietly replied, "Would you mind if I try the fly rod for awhile?"

During the next three hours Joe caught as many bass as I did—and this was on waters that I was fishing constantly. Around noon we decided to have lunch and pulled the canoe up on a large rock ledge in the middle of the Potomac River. After a pleasant half hour of eating and conversation, Joe looked upstream from the rock. The water was slick and the breeze had died. The surface was dimpled with small rings. Joe picked up his rod, tied on a Black Ghost streamer, and walked to the upriver side of the ledge. I followed, curious and not knowing what to expect.

Joe stripped off the thick line and began working his bamboo rod back and forth. We saw a rise appear and Joe dropped the fly inches above it. One or two pulls on the line and a smallmouth hit the fly. It crashed out of the water as Joe lifted the rod and within a short time he landed the fish. During the next fifteen or twenty minutes Joe caught a bass almost every other cast. It was like picking apples from a tree. I was enthralled and from that moment I knew I had to learn how to fly fish.

The experience of watching Joe changed my life. Joe and I became very close friends, and he was like a second Dad to me (my own father died when I was six.) He had a great deal to do with my entry into the outdoor writing field. More than introducing me to fly fishing, Joe taught me many of the principles that have guided me since then. Aside from meeting Ev, my wife of forty-six years, his was one of the most important relationships in my life.

My evolution into saltwater fly fishing came naturally. The thrill of hooking larger, wilder fish that tested angler and tackle was a challenge I could not ignore. Because I lived close to Chesapeake Bay, my first encounters were with striped bass, which Marylanders call "rockfish." In the 1950s there were so many around it was mind boggling. I wanted a fly that had the shape of a baitfish, swam well, and when cast into the air would offer little resistance. I tinkered with fly designs and came up with the Lefty's Deceiver.

During the 1950s I made several exploratory trips to New England, New Jersey, the Florida Keys, and the Outer Banks of North Carolina. Again it was Joe Brooks who fired me to a white heat, this time over saltwater fly fishing. When Castro took over Cuba, he hired Joe to bring a number of outdoor writers there, so they could sample the fishing and go home and write about it. I was one of the first people Joe called. We were taken to Cayo Galinda, on the north coast of Cuba. I waded the clear waters armed with a South Bend Fiberglass rod and a GAF line that had been spooled on my first fly reel, a Pflueger Medalist. Near a mangrove shoot, I saw a small silvery shadow that I thought was a bonefish. I had cast to them before but never caught one. I dropped my fly ten feet in front of the fish, stripped, and the bonefish surged forward. In a rush it grabbed the fly, and after I set the hook the fish took off on what has been my most astonishing moment in fishing— ever! It was difficult to control the whining reel, though I used my fingertips on the inside of the spool flange to try to slow the fish. I shall never forget the end of that first run. I could see something splashing more than 125 yards in the distance. I had great difficulty comprehending that the bonefish I had just hooked was already so far away! Twenty minutes later I finally landed that bonefish. That "small fish" turned out to weigh ten pounds.

Despite all the species that I have caught since then, the bonefish is my favorite. I believe it is perfect fly rod quarry, offering the most difficulty when it comes down to

LEFTY KREH AND STU APTE WITH HUGE TARPON   *STU APTE*

"...you simply have to be a better fisherman to be successful in saltwater."

catch-per-cast ratio. Many things have to be correct—the cast, timing, tackle, presentation. Make one small mistake and the game is over.

I confess that when I caught my first giant tarpon in the Keys, I thought this had to be the pinnacle of the sport. A few years later I was able to fish with Kirk Smith, Dr. Dee Mitchell, and Harold LeMaster at Homosassa, Florida. These three men had been fishing for the unusually large tarpon there for years and let me in on the secret. It was awesome to see so many huge fish. Since we never saw anyone else, the fish were undisturbed and we caught them with great frequency. One day, I boated a tarpon while fishing with Dee Mitchell, that, according to a tape measurement, weighed 208 pounds. I refused to bring it in, fearing that others would flock to the spot. We did take a picture of the portion of the fish that Dee could hold above the water. Unfortunately, two years later the secret was out. Homosassa became "crowded" and I set out to explore other parts of the world.

During my years of fly fishing I have seen a great many incredible things. Sailfishing was something that especially blew my mind. To witness such a monster fish, its sail raised in fury just yards behind the boat, is a special fly-fishing moment. In Northern Australia, I also watched with awe as a fifty pound Spaniard mackerel sky-rocketed thirty feet through the air while trying to dislodge my hook. I carried line friction burns on my fingers for two weeks after fighting the Nuigini black bass, the strongest fish, I believe, that swims. Yet, as much joy as I feel for all kinds of fly fishing, if I had one day left to fish, I'd want to go after bonefish.

I know one thing for certain: you simply have to be a better fisherman to be successful in saltwater. There is always a wind demanding that you cast well, and tackle has to be in top-flight condition. Everything in saltwater is being eaten by something bigger than itself. The only escape most fish have is to swim away. That means their speed and endurance is vastly superior to fresh-water species. Lastly, in many saltwater fishing situations you also must cast within a few seconds of seeing a fish and your cast must be accurate. This requires much greater skill than most fresh-water fishermen have mastered.

Fly fishing has allowed me to meet so many wonderful people. I've fished for everything with all sorts of tackle, from offshore trolling gear, to carp fishing with dough balls. And maybe it sounds prejudiced, but I <u>know</u> that fly fishermen are a little different from all other anglers. Fly fishermen enjoy helping others who share the sport; they seem to enjoy the camaraderie rather than the competition. Many of the nicest people that I have met in my life have been introduced to me through my fly fishing experiences. Fly fishermen, more than any other type of anglers, have led the fight to protect the species and clean up our waters.

Some people are astonished at how many CEOs, doctors, and people who have reached the top in their stressful careers, are fly fishermen, especially saltwater fly fishermen. I understand completely. Nothing you can do is as relaxing as going fly fishing—though at the same time it requires total concentration and careful preparation to be successful.

A very pleasant event in fly fishing during the past two decades has been the increasing number of women who are joining the sport. Fly fishing attracts women because it is a noncompetitive but challenging sport that takes place in beautiful surroundings. The camaraderie of the sport comes easily because "fly fishers" tend to be well read, good conversationalists, and fun to be with.

8

FLORIDA KEYS   *CHICO FERNANDEZ*

*"Almost everything about saltwater
fly fishing is exquisite…"*

BRIAN O'KEEFE

NEAL ROGERS

> *"Fly fishing attracts women because it is a noncompetitive but challenging sport that takes place in beautiful surroundings."*

Almost everything about saltwater fly fishing is exquisite. Saltwater fish come in every hue from cobalt blue to liquid silver. Blazing color is everywhere. To be moving slowly along offshore and see the skin of the dark-blue ocean fractured as a school of fish or squid leap above the surface, attempting to escape the brightly colored predators below, makes the blood race. In shore, a coral reef has to be one of God's great art works. Here is life at its very best—pristine and teeming with myriads of species. One of the most enjoyable experiences for me now is to take someone who has never been there to a shallow tropical flat. Looking through polarizing glasses opens the fisherman's eyes and expands the flats fishing experience to another dimension. I have visited nowhere else on this earth where you can see so many gorgeous colors of water as on a tropical flat; the brilliant white of the sand and the multitude of shades of pink through turquoise, in addition to the play of the wind and clouds, the sun and the tropical foliage, creates a combination that is always changing and always stunningly beautiful. Whether wading or moving along in a boat, fishing with any kind of tackle, a saltwater flat offers more visual treats than almost any other place I know. And nowhere else can you get so close to truly large fish in such clear water.

Someone once asked me at a seminar why I went fly fishing. Many reasons popped into my mind, but one stood out above all others. "One thing, I guess, is that you fly fish in the most beautiful places."

This is the chief reason for this book. It shows us that marvelous, magical, and beautiful world of saltwater fly fishing. ☐

"*…nowhere else can you get so close to truly large fish in such clear water.*"

BILLY RABITO

NEAL ROGERS

12

SUNRISE—FLORIDA KEYS

NEAL ROGERS

CONTENTS

13

A HISTORY OF MODERN SALTWATER FLY FISHING

By Stu Apte

STU APTE – 1948

When Neal and Linda Rogers asked me to write a personal history of saltwater fly fishing the task seemed pretty simple—start at the beginning and tell who did what, and when. But this history happened without some addled writer standing by taking notes. The first angler didn't bother to notify *Salt Water Sportsman*, *Field & Stream*, or *Outdoor Life*. He just tied a glob of deer hair and feathers onto a hook and tried to fool some wild ocean fish into thinking it was the main course. All the great anglers know the sport from A to Z. Modern anglers are meteorologists, seamen, mechanics, explorers, casters, fly tiers, and artists, and revere the environment. All of which means, if I have left anybody out, it is definitely an oversight.

Fly fishing in saltwater has had a quirky sort of evolution. Starting with gear designed for trout or trolling, we had to grope our way through a maze of tackle, figure out the most effective knots, how to use it all, then agree on a set of rules to tell us how well we were doing. Eventually we graduated from the age-old split bamboo and gossamer, and rushed into space-age plastic, but the basic ingredient remained: the predator's urge to conjur up a sporting challenge between man and fish, with a bit of grace and a touch of ancient art.

I was born and raised in Miami, grew up fishing in the neighbor's goldfish pond, then Biscayne Bay, and, as a teenager, won a couple of divisions of the famous Metropolitan Miami Fishing Tournament (MET). I was lucky enough then to meet and fish with some of the world's finest anglers and gentlemen. Joe Brooks became my mentor. We fished a lot together, and teamed up later in films and TV specials as angler and guide. Though I decided to design my life to allow "enough" time for fishing, I could never get enough. I fished for bonefish off Miami, I hunted the canals for baby tarpon and the back country of the Keys for snook, redfish, anything that would bust a lure. I thought someday I'd be a fishing guide, the most personally rewarding and fun occupation I could imagine.

I often dream of my boyhood days in the 1940s. I'd go out on the Venetian Causeway, right downtown, stalking snook, ladyfish, and small tarpon. There was no pollution in Biscayne Bay then, or even in the Miami River. My first fly rod was a split bamboo South Bend 49, the reel an Ocean City Plymouth, third-hand, with a level "C" line. While a student at the University of Miami, I camped out on the causeway to catch daybreak, when the monster jack crevalle came marauding in from the ocean, busting mullet along the seawall before the sun boiled up. My mother was sure there was "something wrong with that boy!"

Fishing was my early obsession. I gave every spare minute to my popping bugs, streamers, and click reels-Pflueger Medalists, mostly. With that early type of gear, the fish would really tear up my fingers. Then, as now, I'd fight fish with the line running between my fingers, to gauge the exact amount of drag I wanted.

Back then, bonefish were easier. One day I was using a plug called "Leaping Lena," trying for a big barracuda I knew was there. While working the "Florida Whip," or "walking the dog," zig-zagging, I had a tremendous strike and immediately set the hook. I had to wade out deeper and deeper in order to keep from losing all my line. Finally, landed, the fish proved to be a nine-pound -fourteen ounce bonefish. It won the MET that year. Unheard of, a bonefish had crashed a topwater plug!

I tied flies to make money to buy fishing gear during my high school and college years, and probably supplied more bonefish flies for tackle shops than all the manufacturers combined. They were just simple bucktails. By calling them "bonefish flies" I got a good price. There were a few Keys guides back then who fished with the fly—Jimmy Albright, Cecil Keith, Bill Smith, Rolie and Hollie Hollenbeck, George Hommel, and Jimmy's wife, Frankee Albright. All have made their mark—you see their names on special knots, and Hommel was President Bush's guide when he came to fish Islamorada. As a teen, when I'd drive through Islamorada, I'd crane my neck hoping to get a glimpse of Jimmy Albright, my idol. The big tarpon he produced for some of his clients just lit my fire.

Things were more primitive back in the late 1940s. It was a time of magical exploration in the Florida Keys, the golden years of un-touched waters. I was a teenager, driving down from Miami with Joe Brooks. We parked along narrow, two-laned US 1 in upper Key Largo, at Garden Cove. A few hundred yards from the ocean, the pathway ran through a dense tangle of gumbo limbo, buttonwood, and mangroves. It was dank and dark, even at mid-day, dripping humidity. We stumbled down the jungle path, running all out, reeking of citronella, but still black with ravenous mosquitos, flailing away, struggling to get across the coral. Finally we broke out to waterside, and we could see them out there tailing—bonefish that had never seen a fly. As I waded out to cast, I knew it was worthwhile to run that awful gauntlet. These were special times for Joe and myself. We felt like explorers, the first sampling the legendary places of the Keys. Obviously we weren't the first, but the place was so empty that it sure felt like it.

Of course, somebody started before that. A. L. Dimmock is probably the most famous because he was photographed extensively while trolling feathers for tarpon in the 1890s. He wasn't aware of our modern classic fly rules. "You must cast and retrieve your fly in the orthodox manner." He used a two-handed salmon rod and long wire leaders. I'd have to admit it was sporting, though. He fished from a canoe. It was especially exciting when the large sharks would chase the tarpon into the canoe at Bahia Honda. His photographic records of the Keys and the fishing were incredible.

Around 1946, right after World War II, it became a fad to use flies for snook out on the Tamiami Trail between Everglade City and the Marco Island turnoff. Homer Rhodes, Jr., was commercial fishing snook out there—a fly rod produced more for him than plugs. Fly fishing for bonefish, redfish, and tarpon was becoming the "in thing" for tourists. But there were no standards, not much in the line of rules to judge your catch by, and the equipment was certainly lacking. The Miami Beach Rod & Reel Club, and the MET drew up the early standards for saltwater fly fishing. The Rod & Reel Club had a category called "Fly Light," with the fly attached directly to the leader tippet, and "Fly Heavy," which allowed twelve inches of trace material, wire or heavy mono, to protect against toothy fish. The sole line test then was twelve pound tippet.

Around that time the modern movement of saltwater fly fishing got going, with anglers like Joe Brooks, who was also manager of the MET, and A.J. McClane, Angling Editor of *Field & Stream*, and author of *McClane's Fishing Encyclopedia*, and, of course, Ted Williams of Boston Red Sox fame.

In the late 1940s and early 1950s plastics came to saltwater fly fishing and the new monofilament leaders changed things. It was thinner and less visible to fish. This wonder material called for a whole new series of knots, which we spent hours developing and testing.

In June, 1947, in Miami, Red Greb gave Joe Brooks a streamer fly with barred rock wings, tied on a 1/0 hook. Joe said he was on his way to see if a bonefish would take a fly, and told Red that he would give his fly a try. Down in the Keys, Joe went out on the bonefish flats with Captain Jimmy Albright and took the first two tailing bonefish ever caught on a fly.

It's true that a few bonefish had been landed earlier on flies, but they were incidental catches while fishing for other species of fish. Twenty years earlier Colonel L. S. Thompson of Redbank, New Jersey, had fished Long Key Bight with Captain J. T. Harrod as his guide. They used bait in the orthodox bonefishing way. Then at high tide the Colonel would take up his fly rod, put on a #6 Royal Coachman wet fly, and cast to the edges of the mangroves for baby tarpon. He caught tarpon up to five pounds and twice landed bonefish. They thought of these catches as accidental so when the tide went out, the Colonel and his guide poled back to the flats and fished bait again for the tailing and cruising bonefish.

In the early 1940s Captain Bill Smith also took a bonefish on a fly. No one followed up until that day in June 1947 when Joe took those two tailers. As far as is known, they were the first bonefish ever taken by an angler deliberately fishing for them with a fly. Joe's success started a stampede. Anglers soon heard about the thrills of taking bonefish on flies—stalking a fish across the flats, dropping a fly in front of it without scaring it, watching it follow the fly, coaxing it to hit, and then trying to keep it on during the sensational run a bonefish makes when hooked on fly tackle.

Just about the time the Florida flats were becoming popular, along came the Korean War and changed my dream. I discovered a second love—flying. I joined the Navy in 1951 to become an Aviation Cadet, and ended up flying fighter planes off carriers. My entry into the serious part of saltwater fly fishing was delayed. When I got out of the service in December 1955, I wanted to fish and I wanted to fly. There was a shortage of airline pilots, so I was wooed by the major airlines. Pan Am was perfect for me—they flew to those exotic places with great fishing, and I'd have time off between the long hauls so I could (ahem) have my fish and eat it, too. In 1957 I was laid off. I decided to go back to my first love—I'd get a license to be a backcountry fishing guide. I made my living then as a guide in the Keys, just as the modern era of saltwater fly fishing was gaining momentum.

In the early 1960s Dr. Webb Robinson of Key West caught the first billfish on a fly r Panama. He caught a striped mar in at Baja in 1962. Web trolled hockless teasers and had the captain put the boat into neutral so he could cast and retrieve properly.

The second billfish, a sail, was taken by J. Lee Cuddy, a well-known angler, and a member of the Miami Beach Rod & Reel Club. I caught the third one, but not until 1964 at Club de Pesca de Panama, now called Tropic Star Lodge. News of this really got the angling world excited.

Rods back then when we first got into Fiberglass, were very soft. In the early 1960s we were using G2AF lines (10 weight). In 1964 I fished a G3AF, equivalent to an 11 weight rod, in Panama when I caught the third sailfish—eighty-seven pounds.

To catch that fish I used a Rogue reel made in Grant's Pass, Oregon. This reel was designed for steelhead and Pacific salmon, and was made of cast aluminum. The Rogue did have a disc-drag system that worked well. (I still have a couple of them.) The Rogue reel certainly was not the quality of the Fin Nor "wedding cake," Seamaster, or Bogdan fly reels. I guess an interesting point that can be made here is that you should do the best you can with the equipment that is available. The longest standing saltwater fly rod record to date is my 58 pound dolphin caught in 1964 on this same Rogue reel. In 1965 I managed a 128-pound sailfish on an original Seamaster reel, and then a 136-pound sailfish (still the record) using a #3 Fin Nor "wedding cake." In order to get 225 yards of backing on my reels it was necessary for me to cut my fly line back to 85 feet.

In 1960 and 1961 I did a couple of films with Lee Wulff on catching

16

big tarpon. I had booked a week over the full moon tides of May, 1961 to guide Dick Wolf, Vice President of Garcia Fishing Tackle Corp., to shoot a film titled "FLY RODDING BIG TARPON." While Lee and Dick were unpacking their clothing at the old Vista Linda Hotel on Big Pine Key, I scrutinized their fly-fishing equipment, wanting to make sure they had everything properly rigged. Well, to cut a long story short, I spent most of that night pulling fly lines and backing off of all their reels and re-doing all of the connections. Lee, of course, was Mr. Atlantic Salmon, but had never before fished for tarpon. I have always been known for telling it like it is, and I guess our first meeting would not be considered a Public Relations dream. But, as they say, all's well that ends well. Lee shot an award-winning film, Dick Wolf landed a 132 pound tarpon, and Lee and I became good friends with a great deal of mutual respect. We later collaborated on a second film.

As a guide I'd try to produce record catches for my clients. Back in those days it was easier to produce record catches as the tarpon and bonefish of the lower Florida Keys had hardly been fished. More often than not, a reasonable cast with a fly would be rewarded with a take. Then if your knots held and lady luck was looking over your shoulder, you had your reward.

In the early 1960s Joe Brooks' fly rod record tarpon of 148½ pounds yanked me out of the boat twice as I gaffed it. Joe usually fished a 9½ foot Orvis Battenkill rod with the equivalent of a 10 weight line and fly light tipet. But, good luck or bad, I had stepped on his rod tip and broken it. He used my heavy glass rod fully rigged with fly heavy to take the record.

One favorite client, Ray Donnersberger of Highland Park, Illinois, won the Tarpon Fly Division of the MET for four years in a row. It was April 1962 in the lower Florida Keys. Ray, for the past hour, had been hooked up to a tarpon we both wanted badly. Ray and I were both driven by the desire to win the MET Fly Division for tarpon. I knew this fish would be a contender for the all-time fly rod record in the MET. Ray was fishing with a new type of glass fly rod, and this definitely was not the time for experimenting. I know of no man I would rather have had in my boat fighting that fish. Ray was 6'4" and weighed only about 180 pounds, but he moved like a cat and battled the fish as if his life depended upon it. He was and still is a top-notch fly caster, a fantastic person, a great conservationist, a naturalist, and all-around sportsman. I wasn't worried about losing that big tarpon.

The day had been flat calm when we neared Loggerhead Bank and first spotted a school of about eighty tarpon daisy-chaining on the surface. As I poled near the school Ray presented his fly to a large fish. He made his cast just to the outside of the circle so that on the retrieve his fly would move in the same direction as the fish and would not alarm them. The tarpon took the fly eagerly, but too much grass floating on the surface made the fight a difficult one. Finally the moment of truth was at hand.

When it comes time to gaff a big tarpon, or any large fish, it is important that you have a rod with sufficient butt strength to lift his head. I was ready with the gaff as Ray worked the fish into position. As

ABOVE: JOE BROOKS AND ROCKY WEINSTEIN ADMIRING A TAMIAMI SNOOK.   *LEFTY KREH PHOTO*

17

LEFT: CAPTAIN BOB McCHRISTIAN BUILDER OF SEAMASTER REELS
        BOB STEARNS PHOTO

BELOW: LEE WULFF WITH A ONE-HUNDRED-POUND-PLUS FLORIDA KEYS TARPON—1960s   *STU APTE PHOTO*

STU APTE PULLED OVERBOARD BY JOE BROOKS' WORLD RECORD TARPON   *STU APTE PHOTO*

I made my move. Ray exerted a bit more pressure than that thin-walled stick had to offer, and it literally exploded into six pieces, just as I struck the tarpon. I had gaffed that fish at the same instant the rod blew. The MET rules stated that a broken rod disqualifies a catch. Did the rod break before or after the fish had been caught? Ray, being the sportsman that he is, refused to claim the fish, even though it was three pounds heavier than the MET record at that time.

In 1967 I took a friend from Palm Beach, Guy de La Valdene, to learn fly fishing for tarpon. We were in the lower Florida Keys to fish the full moon tides of April. The weather was perfect, a gentle southeast breeze of eight to ten mph with just an occasional fair-weather cumulus cloud that could block our visibility. The tide had been flooding for two hours when we began to see a number of tarpon rolling in a nearby channel. I had positioned my skiff, "Mom's Worry," on a flat that I code-named "Bullfighter's " because it was near Big Spanish Key. I could see a school of about forty tarpon coming our way. "Be ready to cast to ten o'clock," I instructed Guy. As soon as the leading fish were in range, he false cast once and then shot out the yellow-and-orange streamer. Though it landed a little off target, a very big fish peeled from the school and came after it. I remember holding my breath, waiting for a strike that I knew should be more like an explosion.

But in his excitement, and from inexperience, too, I suppose, Guy struck too soon and took the fly away from that huge gaping mouth. "Cast again!" I shouted. This time the fly fell closer to the tail end of the school, and a small fish grabbed it. Guy did a good job fighting and landing his first tarpon ever, about a sixty-pounder.

Guy said, laughing, "Now you take the rod and cast to the next tarpon we see so that you can show me what you've been talking about." I didn't have long to wait. The boat had drifted only a short distance when I spotted a school of forty or fifty tarpon cruising just out of casting range. The water was calm, and I knew they would be spooky, so I crouched to cut the size of my silhouette against the sky. In that position I waited. The lead fish was a large one, but a much larger tarpon swam near the center of the pack. Still, I decided to make my presentation to the first fish rather than risk having my line fall across other tarpon and spook all of them.

I cast my yellow-and-orange saddle hackle streamer (which, incidentally had been tied for me by Larry Kreh, Lefty's fourteen year-old son) in the path of the pack and briefly let it settle. As the lead fish approached, I began the retrieve. The leader charged after it for about ten feet, then started to turn away. I stopped the fly. I can still remember the butterflies that danced in my stomach. The tarpon came back, I twitched the fly, and she had it. The first run, interrupted by two jumps, was short and only stripped off the thirty yards of fly line and a bit of backing. I figured the fish's weight at about 120 pounds. After the fish's first run, I remember turning to Guy and suggesting that he take the rod and fight the fish, just to gain experience. "No thanks," he said. "I'll just relax and watch the pro."

Though I didn't know it at the time, Guy's reply was the second biggest break of the whole trip for me. The first was his earlier suggestion that I cast while he poled the boat. This tarpon topped the scale at 151 pounds, besting Joe Brooks' world record on 12 pound tippet.

Four years later, in April, I was back flying airplanes for Pan Am, and Ray and I were now fishing as buddies. By 1:45 p.m. we had launched my boat at Garrison Bight in Key West in order to catch an outgoing tide flowing off an old favorite tarpon bank. By 3:00 p.m. I had presented my fly to a tarpon. Ray had been poling the boat downwind to the south. I remember my best visibility was east, off to my left. We were in about eight feet of water. As I searched the area carefully I became aware of a greenish hue to the water that blended with the dark green bottom, but was somehow different. I guessed it was tarpon, so I turned and took an eighty foot upwind shot. I worked the fly once by stripping line and had an immediate strike. I saw the tarpon, about a sixty-pounder, but when I tried to set the hook, he was gone. I picked up, making my backcast downwind and tried a second presentation to that greenish area I now knew for sure was a school of tarpon. The fly landed six or seven feet downwind of where the main part of the school had moved. As I started stripping line I remarked to Ray, "I don't believe I got back to them." No sooner were the words out of my mouth than I watched a tarpon come over—its entire head out of water—and engulf that fly. I waited just for a moment before setting the hook and got only a slight glimpse of the tarpon's first jump, as I was busy clearing my fly line. The fish made a sizzling run toward deeper water and jumped again about one hundred yards out. Even at that distance I could tell it was a huge fish.

The next half hour was grueling. Ray kept the boat on top of the fish, which was now in about twenty feet of water. Once when the tarpon rose up to gulp air, we almost got a shot with the gaff. This fish was looking bigger all the time. We came near a shallow bar in the middle of the channel. Twice I thought the fish might cross it and I had Ray cut the engine. As we drifted onto the bar I was able to persuade the tarpon to stay with us. At this point probably forty minutes had gone by and both the big fish and I were tired. In this shallow water I got my first good look at the tarpon. It was monstrous! The water next to the boat was almost too shallow for such a big fish to swim in. I spent the next ten minutes trying to persuade that fish to come in closer. At last I had him beside the boat and Ray braced himself for a shot with the two-handed gaff. Ray had never gaffed a tarpon before, yet he deftly slipped it under the tarpon and drove the point home. The fish gave one big shake and was quiet. I grabbed a lip gaff and put in the huge mouth and, for the first time, felt the trophy was mine. We wasted no time getting off the bar and made a fast run to the Key West Yacht Club, nearest Official Weighing Station for the MET. At 4:15 p.m. on April 10, 1971, we officially recorded the vital satistics of a new world record fly rod tarpon-weight 154 pounds; length 79 inches; girth 44 inches. The leader tippet later tested at 10.8 pounds. I had set the new fly rod tournament record for the MET—and a world record to boot. Years before when I had worked as a guide I had often remarked that given the choice of having the most skillful angler as a customer or the luckiest, I would take the luckiest every time. I was sure at that time that I was that luckiest angler.

The largest tarpon on a fly at this writing is 188 pounds on 17 1/2 pound-test tippet, caught by William Pate, Jr. This fish approaches the wild dream of every fly rod afficionado—the ever- elusize, near-mythical, but very real 200-pound monster.

Every April, May, and June when the big Mamoos come into the shallows in the Keys and Homossasa Springs, the fly fishing heavy-weights also gather, hoping to be the first to land "The Legend." They could soon be surprised, however, by news from the newest giant hot spot—Africa—where the average fish is much larger—and more innocent. Photojournalist Brian O'Keefe set a new 10 kg. record with a 187-pounder at Sierra Leone. Our saltwater fly rod mania has spread throughout the world. At first we explored the near waters of Belize, Mexico, Costa Rica, and Panama, but now South America, Africa, New Zealand, and Australia entice us, as well.

New ideas have also brought an evolution of fly gear, knots, lines, and techniques. Dr. Webb Robinson and Lee Cuddy originated the concept of teasing fish up to hit a fly. In Panama, 1964, at Tropic Star Lodge, we caught bonito and rigged hookless belly baits, trolling them to get the big sails interested. When a sail or marlin came up slashing, the teaser rod handler let them mouth it to excite and bring the fish into casting range. With the fish fifty or sixty feet out, I'd yell for the captain to take the engine out of gear. He'd answer, "Neutral," and on my command the teaser was jerked away from the fish. I'd cast the popping bug close to the billfish, now mad as a hornet, and it would crash the fly. Then all hell would break loose—screaming reels, grey-hounding leaps, and anglers in a state of excited mania! It's a bit of a con game, sure, where the Artful Dodger uses a ruse to convince the excited sail

LEAPING TARPON OFF COSTA RICA   *STU APTE PHOTO*

DOC ROBINSON AND CAPTAIN LEFTY REGAN (WITH CIGAR) WITH THE FIRST MARLIN EVER CAUGHT BY FLY-CASTING—A 145-POUNDER.
FROM VIC DUNAWAY

LEFTY KREH, MARK SOSIN & STU APTE—DEMONSTRATING FLYCASTING

C. BOYD PFEIFFER PHOTO

that a clump of deer hair and chicken feathers is good to eat. But presentation and technique are as important in fly fishing as is flashy equipment.

We had a lot of fun figuring out how to hook a wahoo in the "classic manner." At Club Pacifico in Panama every summer and fall, wahoo run in schools. In 1974 George Hommel, Billy Pate, and Carl Navarre tried all sorts of ways to take a wahoo on a fly. The fish is very fast moving and smart, and has excellent eyesight; they turned down all the flies those expert anglers offered. The problem was that a wahoo would hit a teaser, tear it to shreds or pull so hard it would be out of range in an instant. To keep the fish close to the boat, they tied the flat line to the transom and trolled a securely tied hooked bait. The wahoo would smack the bait, but would tear the hook out of its mouth on the sizzling first run. The anglers had very little time to get the fly out there, and then even holding the rod under one arm and stripping with both hands couldn't interest the critter to strike. The following season Bob Griffin, the club owner, had an idea. He towed a long bungee cord off the stern with a 120-pound mono leader and a piece of wire with a Japanese feather hooked to it. He trolled it fast, 45 to 50 feet behind the boat. I stood by, fly rod in hand. The wahoo loved Griffin's rig. It charged the bungee-trolled feather until it hooked up. That fish would zip back and forth wildly, lighting up its buddies. With the boat in neutral, I cast a tarpon fly and made a normal strip. They fought each other to get at my fly. In one day, with the help of Griffin's rig, we set all four of the wahoo records on a fly. Innovation, within a set of regulations and parameters, adds to the growth of the sport.

Other fish, like dolphin (mahi mahi), aren't choosy. On that same Panama trip for my first billfish, we saw a big mahogany tree floating off the mouth of the Jaque River. We eased over to see what was under it. The captain hollered "Big Dorado, Señor." I could see the electric blue-green pectoral fins. The captain backed down the single-screw diesel to within sixty feet of the tree, and I cast a popping bug with a 2/0 hook. The smallest of the three fish zoomed up to slurp it. This wild jumper weighed fifty-nine pounds and is still the longest standing saltwater fly rod record. It was caught on twelve pound test tippet. The other two, I estimate, were in the seventy and one hundred pound range.

Permit are another story. In the early days it was exasperating to try to take a permit on a fly. These rascals would always prevent you from achieving a classic "Grand Slam" in saltwater fly fishing—a bonefish, a tarpon, and a permit. The permit would reject almost everything. They'd charge the fly or totally ignore it. Once in a while they would finally strike and give the frustrated angler a major surprise. Innovative tiers put in a hundred thousand man hours to

PIERRE AFFRE PHOTO

lengths, weight test, and so forth, to get the most out of your sport. They've evolved over the years, and there is a reason for every one of them.

I see a curious and remarkable quality about fly fishermen. As a breed, we need to know there are regulations to satisfy ourselves we've done it right. I understand that need. If someone else doesn't, he might as well use big trolling tackle. Or live bait. Dynamite may take more fish than feather, but it's not art. The art is playing this game in the classic manner. The rules in the early years came from the Saltwater Fly Rodders of America, in Toms River, New Jersey. Their Advisory Board was a Who's Who of Fly Fishing— people like Frank Woolner and Hal Lyman of *Salt Water Sportsman*, Joe Brooks, of course, A. J. McClane, Charlie Waterman, Lefty Kreh and Mark Sosin, who kept the records, Lee Wulff, and myself. This Board studied the needs and set the rules. Later, the International Game Fish Association (IGFA) became the governing body, and it still is today.

Initially, records were kept only for twelve pound tippet. No matter if it was a ten pound bonefish, one hundred pound tarpon, or three hundred pound marlin, it had to be taken on twelve pound or less. If you caught it on four pound tippet it was still twelve pound class. Today, those weight tests have evolved into kg. classes, starting at 1 kg., which is approximately 2.2 pounds, and there are 2 kg., 4kg., 6 kg., 8 kg., and 10 kg. categories.

So we've come through forty or fifty years of saltwater fly fishing, strung together with a Homer Rhodes Loop, an Albright Knot, and a bit of a Bimini Twist. The Hufnagle Knot is being used now along with space age plastics, graphite rods, and exquisitely designed reels. We all anxiously await the perfect rod and reel that will lay out one hundred feet of line in any wind and have the fly land on the water like a feather.

I get great satisfaction reminiscing about the wonderful moments I've experienced in saltwater fly fishing. My earlier tackle has been retired to a glass display case in my home. My first Seamaster reel, still rigged with a GBF Torpedo Taper, sits proudly in its place of honor. The part it played in this exquisitely intricate sport brings warm memories to my heart.

Innovations will come, and the challenge, in this strange and wonderful confrontation between man and fish, will persevere. It takes only a bit of sporting grace and a touch of ancient art. ☐

develop flies that look exactly like the permit's favorite food, small crabs. So on the right day, today, a good angler might release two or more permit on a fly.

There are some lures that are not really flies because you can't false cast them or "cast and retrieve them in the orthodox manner." That's one of the rules that makes this a truly great sport. To be a real participant, you have to abide by the rules for casting, shock tippet

EAST & WEST COASTS OF NORTH AMERICA

Migrations of fish up and down the coast bring a variety of species within range of the coastal fisherman. Stripers, blues, redfish, tarpon, bonito, sea bass, sea trout, and salmon are the favorites. Offshore fly fishing for sailfish, marlin, and tuna is still in its infancy, but the catches can be incredible.

There's nothing quite like chasing schools of large fish crashing bait in the surf!

DAN BLANTON

CHRIS FONG

ED JAWOROWSKI

BOB WOLVERTON

ED JAWOROWSKI

ANDY ANDERSON

25

JOEL ARRINGTON

DAN BLANTON

ED JAWOROWSKI

DALE SPARTAS

26

DALE SPARTAS

CHRIS FONG

ED JAWOROWSKI

CHRIS FONG

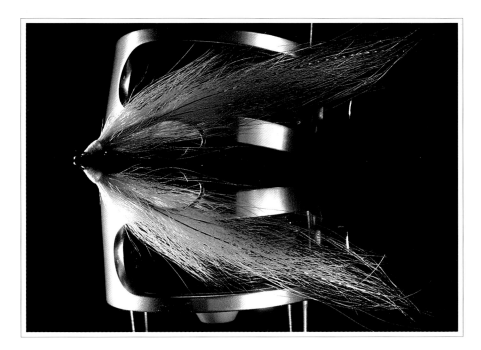

ED JAWOROWSKI

ISLAMORADA

JACK SAMSON

FLORIDA KEYS

NEAL ROGERS

The elemental flatness of the Florida Keys is compelling and mysterious in its thin plane of reflective brilliance. Within their own horizontal galaxy, the flats are as inscrutable as the empyrean-blue water of the Gulf Stream itself, far outside the shoals where you look down along sharp, beveled shafts of light that narrow into blackness thousands of feet above the ocean floor.

Inshore, and out of sight of the Atlantic's barrier reefs, among the very Keys themselves, the horizon is often lost somewhere behind refulgent bands of light and shimmering heat waves. On certain hot, humid days without wind, distant mangrove islands are seen only as extraneous tubes of gray-green, lying inexplicably in the silver atmosphere like alien spaceships.

Over in the backcountry, the Gulf side of the Keys, long plateaus of uneven coral stall the tide and agitate it so the waterscape vibrates and sparkles. The whole of this inside territory is an unfathomably complex tapestry of radical design.

—*Russell Chatham*
from *Silent Seasons*

34

BILLY PATE

KEY WEST

37

DOUBLE TROUBLE

NEAL ROGERS

ANDY ANDERSON

MARATHON

NEAL ROGERS

JOE RICHARD

GIL DRAKE

41

44

45

DAN BLANTON

JEFFREY CARDENAS

CHICO FERNANDEZ

LEFTY KREH   "FLIP"   LEFTY KREH

47

STU APTE

R. VALENT'NE ATKINSON

HA SON CARROLL

MARATHON

NEAL ROGERS

"BILLY"

R. VALENTINE ATKINSON

KEY WEST

JOE RICHARD

CHICO FERNANDEZ

52

SEVEN MILE BRIDGE

NEAL ROGERS

CHICO FERNANDEZ

54

DALE SPARTAS

LEFTY KREH

HANSON CARROLL

BOB STEARNS

BOB STEARNS

WALT STEARNS

TIMOTHY O'KEEFE

58

KEY BISCAYNE

BAHAMA ISLANDS

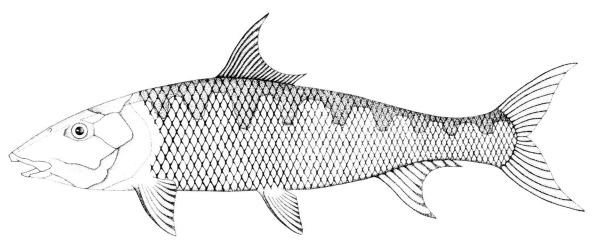

Palm covered islands, turquoise seas and endless white sand flats — this is the Bahamas. Each island in this necklace of jewels has it's own personality. Hey man! Goombay smash, man! Can you hear the reggae?

TIMOTHY O'KEEFE

ANDY ANDERSON

ANDY ANDERSON

BRIAN O'KEEFE

TIMOTHY O'KEEFE

BRIAN O'KEEFE

ANDY ANDERSON

BRIAN O'KEEFE

GIL DRAKE

BRIAN O'KEEFE

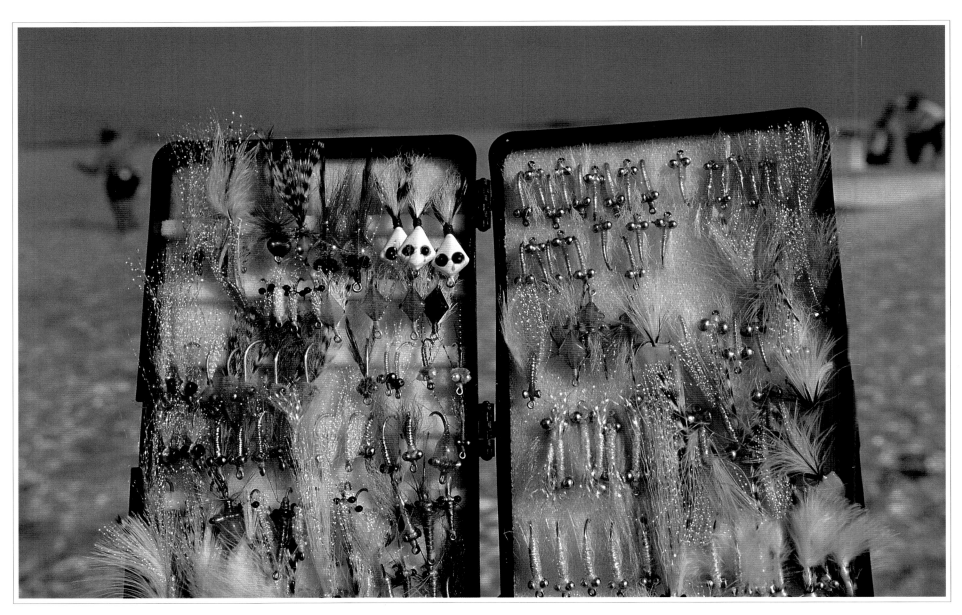

BRIAN O'KEEFE

67

69

GIL DRAKE

NEAL ROGERS

ANDY ANDERSON

TIMOTHY O'KEEFE

BRIAN O'KEEFE

R. VALENTINE ATKINSON

CARIBBEAN SEA—
YUCATAN, BELIZE, HONDURAS, COSTA RICA, VENEZUELA

TONY OSWALD

V ast shallow water flats, laced with deeper channels meandering toward the Atlantic Ocean, are home to bonefish, permit, tarpon, and snook. In this part of the world, the river mouths and their brackish estuaries are an integral part of the ecosystem.

A modern-day adventurer equipped with a reliable boat could spend a lifetime exploring here.

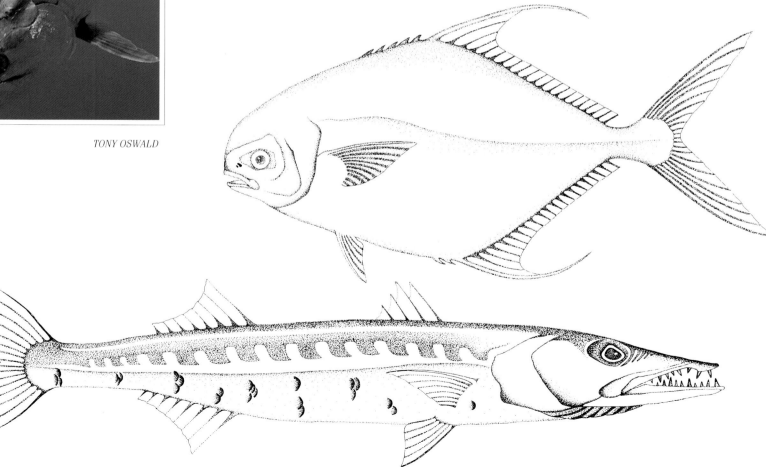

CASA BLANCA

NEAL ROGERS

LINDA ROGERS

LINDA ROGEKS

HONDURAS, ISLAND OF GUANAJA

JOSE AZEL

HONDURAS

CHRIS FONG

DAN BLANTON

BRIAN O'KEEFE

HONDURAS

JOSE AZEL

EL PESCADOR, BELIZE

NEAL ROGERS

82

TURNEFFE ISLANDS, BELIZE

GEORGE ANDERSON

LINDA ROGERS

GEORGE ANDERSON

BELIZE

MIKE WOLVERTON

TONY OSWALD

CASA BLANCA

85

DON CHUEY - CASA BLANCA

EL PESCADOR, BELIZE

BRIAN O'KEEFE

RANDALL KAUFMANN

BRIAN O'KEEFE

CASA BLANCA

MIKE WOLVERTON

NEAL ROGERS

NEAL ROGERS

ASCENSION BAY

R. VALENTINE ATKINSON

BOCA PAILA

R. VALENTINE ATKINSON

LINDA ROGERS

CASA BLANCA   NEAL ROGERS

R. VALENTINE ATKINSON

95

YUCATAN

NEAL ROGERS

DALE SPARTAS

R. VALENTINE ATKINSON

BELIZE CITY

NEAL ROGERS

EL PESCADOR

NEAL ROGERS

BLACKADORE KEY, BELIZE

LINDA ROGERS

97

98

LINDA ROGERS

LOS ROQUES, VENEZUELA

CHICO FERNANDEZ

BOBBI WOLVERTON

LINDA ROGERS

CASA MAR STU APTE   "LEFTY"   DAN BLANTON

EL PESCADOR, BELIZE   LINDA ROGERS

RIO COLORADO RIVER, COSTA RICA

TIMOTHY O'KEEFE

RIO COLORADO, COSTA RICA

NEAL ROGERS

LEFTY KREH

BOBBI WOLVERTON

CASA MAR

NEAL ROGERS

NICK CURCIONE

BILL BARNES

STU APTE

LINDA ROGERS

HARRY KIME

BILL BARNES

BRIAN O'KEEFE

CENTRAL AMERICA – WEST COAST, BAJA

The deep blue waters of the Pacific bring the "Big Boys" of saltwater fly fishing to these shores - sailfish, marlin, tuna, wahoo, and dolphin. Rocky outcroppings along the coast provide perfect habitat for roosterfish as well. This is the place where an angler, armed with modern heavy duty fly tackle can experience what may be the ultimate saltwater confrontation.

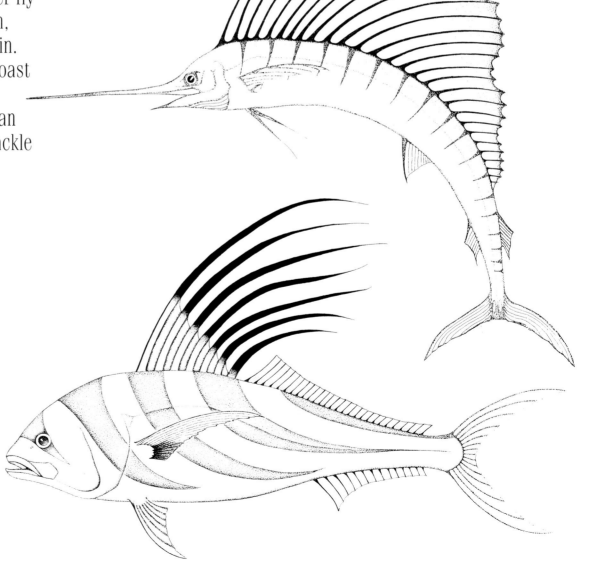

R. VALENTINE ATKINSON

110

LINDA ROGERS

TROPIC STAR, PANAMA

STU APTE

QUEPOS, COSTA RICA

NEAL ROGERS

QUEPOS, COSTA RICA

NEAL ROGERS

MANUEL ANTONIO PARK

NEAL ROGERS

SQUID FLY BY TIM BORSKI   *HANSON CARROLL*

NEAL ROGERS

LINDA ROGERS

NEAL ROGERS

CHRIS FONG

CHRIS FONG

LINDA ROGERS

R . VALENTINE ATKINSON

118

NEAL ROGERS

NEAL ROGERS

QUEPOS, COSTA RICA

NEAL ROGERS

BLUE MARLIN

HANSON CARROLL

MANUEL ANTONIO PARK

NEAL ROGERS

122

123

NEAL ROGERS

LINDA ROGERS

NEAL ROGERS

LINDA ROGERS

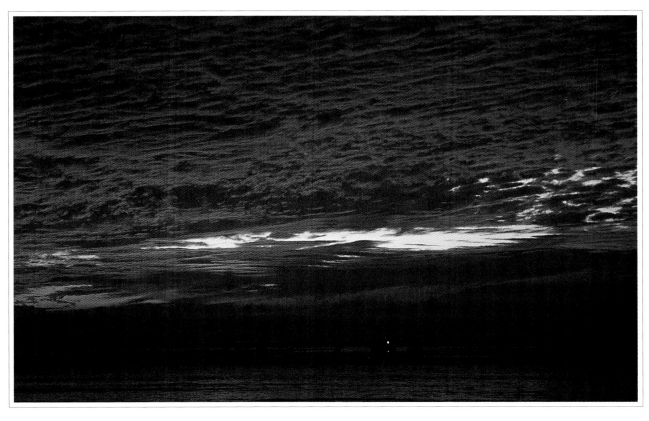

NEAL ROGERS

CABO SAN LUCAS

131

PUNTA ARENAS   LINDA ROGERS   BRIAN O'KEEFE

132

133

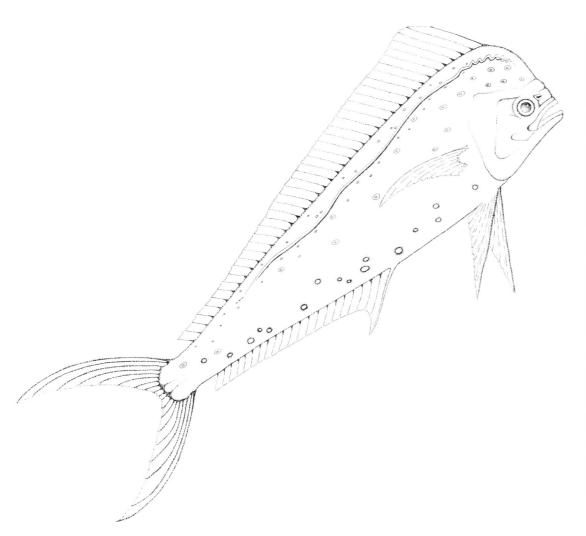

TONY OSWALD

HOTEL CABO SAN LUCAS

BRIAN O'KEEFE

136

WORLDWIDE DESTINATIONS

Where shall we go next? The South Seas, Africa, South America, Asia, Australia - the possibilities are almost endless. Very few of these exotic places have been fished, and even fewer photographed.

Hopefully you will be the lucky one to discover the next fisherman's paradise!

LEFTY KREH

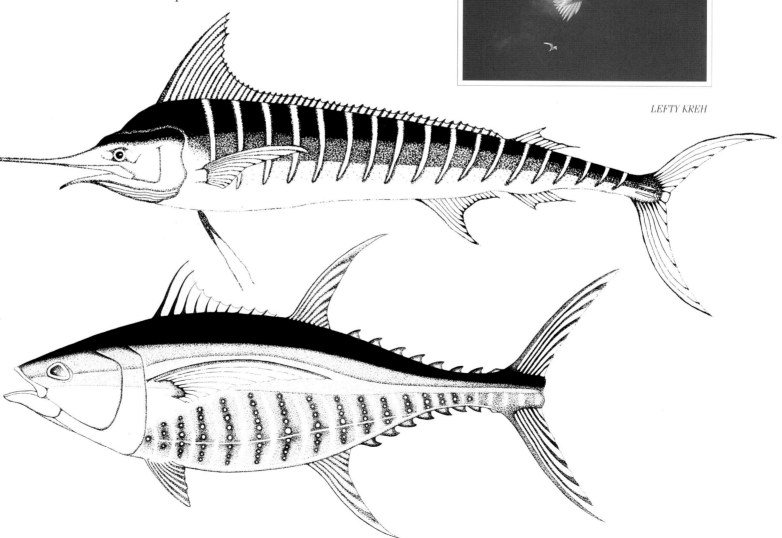

CHRISTMAS ISLAND   *LEFTY KREH*

DAVID STOECKLEIN

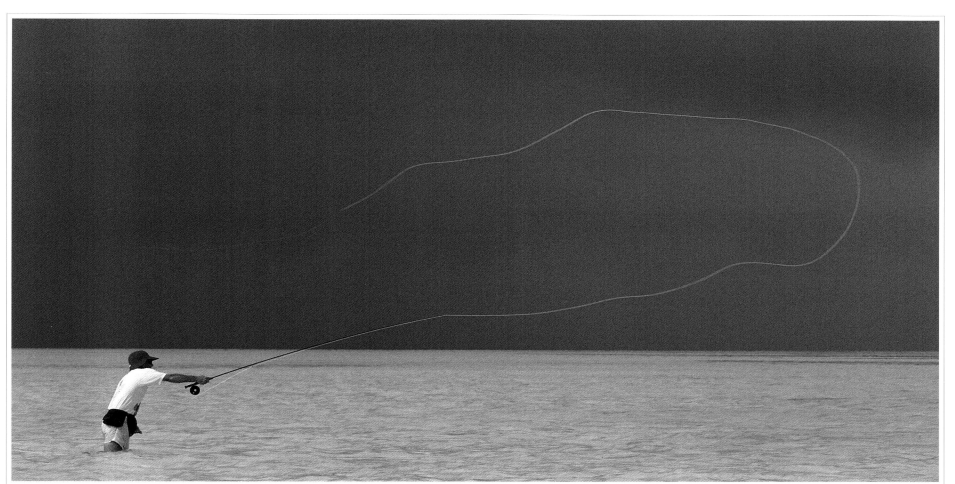

CHRISTMAS ISLAND   *DAVID STOECKLEIN*

DAVID STOECKLEIN

TONGA

BRIAN O'KEEFE

DAVID STOECKLEIN

CHRISTMAS ISLAND

R. VALENTINE ATKINSON

142

ROYAL STAR   *TONY OSWALD*

143

TONY OSWALD   STU APTE   *TONY OSWALD*

TONY OSWALD

"MATCHING THE HATCH" — *TONY OSWALD*

CAIRNS, AUSTRALIA — *ROD HARRISON*

DAKAR, SENEGAL, AFRICA — *TREY COMBS*

ROYAL STAR

TONY OSWALD

BARRAMUNDI - AUSTRALIA

SAM TALARICO

NEW GUINEA

SAM TALARICO

NEW GUINEA

SAM TALARICO

NEW GUINEA

SAM TALARICO

GROUPER - AUSTRALIA

ROD HARRISON

CONTRIBUTING PHOTOGRAPHERS

Craig Rogers

Age: 22

Camera-Film: Minolta, Fuji Velvia

Started fly fishing at age: 7

Craig is the illustrator who portrayed the game fish presented throughout this book.

My present obsession with fish stems back to when I was a young child and my father would take me fishing in the streams and rivers near his house in Montana. Back then I thought fishing was "pretty cool," but I wasn't hooked. Growing up on the streets of Penn Valley, Pennsylvania, the number of times I went fishing were few and far between and the closest thing to fishing that I did with regularity was eating sushi. During my four years at the University of Michigan, my fetish with fish began to flourish and after several fishing trips to the Florida Keys, Belize, and Costa Rica, it became full fledged. Now I dream about fish, I wear one around my neck for good luck, I love to go fishing, I still live for sushi and, of course, I draw pictures of fish. More importantly I live my life by the simple credo, "You can't fish in the same hole for too long," as it applies fittingly to life, love and fishing.

Craig is a freelance artist who specializes in fishing subjects.

1110 Centennial Rd.
Narberth, Pennsylvania 19072
PH: 215-667-2693

Stu Apte

Age: 63

Camera-Film: Nikon, Fuji

Started fly fishing at age: 1940s

Stu Apte is a legend among fisherman all over the world. He's pioneered many new saltwater fly fishing techniques over the past 40 years. We feel very fortunate to have him write about some of his personal experiences in the pages of this book. Stu has probably seen and photographed more magic salt water moments than anyone else we know. Stu's passion for fly fishing the Florida Keys kindled a fire in our hearts 20 years ago. His enthusiasm for fishing started us on a path leading to the production of this book. We just wish we could have been there exploring the Florida Keys with him in the 1950s and 1960s.

Stu holds many fly fishing world records and is best known for his numerous record fly-caught tarpon. Stu wrote *Fishing in the Florida Keys*. He has produced videos, TARPON COUNTRY, SALTWATER FLY FISHING FROM A TO Z, and THE QUEST FOR GIANT TARPON. He helped produce the pilot film for ABC Television's AMERICAN SPORTSMAN, and appeared in WIDE WORLD OF SPORTS with A. J. McLane and Joe Brooks. He is a member of the Fly Fishing Hall of Fame—and was recently elected Worldwide Angler of the Year by the South Island of New Zealand Angling Club for lifetime achievement in fishing and conservation.

Box 87
Gallatin Gateway, Montana 59730
PH: 406-763-4770

Linda Rogers

Age: 43

Camera-Film: Minolta 9xi, Fuji Velvia, 50, 100

Started fly fishing at age: 10

I am one of the fortunate few born and raised in Montana. My father started me out with a spinning rod as soon as I could hold onto one. Fishing the state's lakes, streams, and rivers became an integral part of my life from then on. At about age 10, Dad introduced me to fly fishing, and "I was hooked". I'm one of the few women I know of who received a fly rod and reel for high school graduation from her Dad. I've continued fishing ever since, although now saltwater fly fishing is my main interest.

My parents instilled an appreciation of the world around me as far back as I can remember. It seemed a natural extension of that appreciation for my whole family to get involved with photography to record and preserve the beauty and spectacle around us. Our initial camera was a Brownie box, then an Instamatic. When we really got the bug, we invested in Pentax equipment. For the last 15 years I've used primarily Minolta gear and continue to find great pleasure in my photographic work.

My future goals include catching a "Flats Grand Slam" and touring the back roads of our magnificent country on my Harley with camera ready.

202 South Montana St.
Butte, Montana 59701
PH: 406-723-6526
FX: 406-782-9712

Lefty Kreh

Age: 68

Camera-Film: Nikon, Kodachrome, Fuji

Started fly fishing at age: 10

Lefty is a consummate fisherman. He has amassed more knowledge about the sport than anyone else in the world. He's fished almost everywhere imaginable in fresh and salt water. He never ceases working on the photographic and technical aspects of fishing. A gifted public speaker, Lefty can take a mundane story and make it come alive with humor. He's taught more people the fine art of angling in saltwater through his books and articles than anyone else. We can't thank him enough for his contributions to this book!

Lefty has written articles for all the angling magazines and has authored *Flyfishing in Saltwater* and *Flycasting with Lefty Kreh*. He co-authored (with Mark Sosin) *Practical Fishing Knots*, and *Fishing the Flats*. His new series, *Lefty's Little Library* is immensely popular. Lefty is one of the finest casters in the world and has produced recent videos on flycasting technique. He is a member of the Fly Fishing Hall of Fame.

810 Wickersham Way
Cockeysville, Maryland 21030
PH: 410-667-4876

Neal Rogers

Age: 47

Camera-Film: Nikon F-4, Minolta 9xi-Fuji Velvia, 50, 100

Started fly fishing at age 7

My fly fishing memories date back to 1953 when a dear friend Rose McGuire introduced me to fly tying and fly fishing. I was lucky enough to hook a huge brown trout at Fisherman's Paradise in Pennsylvania. I never landed that fish but he hooked me forever on fly fishing. I was introduced to saltwater by Bill Curtis in 1969. I had a perfect start-four large bonefish in Key Biscayne my first day! Over the years this entire sport has become a poetic art form for me. Everything about it, from nature's splendor through the craftsmanship involved in the tackle gives me a special joy. My photographic skills evolved because of a need I have to capture those special times and share them with everyone. To me the camera is part of the fishing experience. It helps to bring back memories that would otherwise have faded with the passage of time.

The true fun of this sport is the learning process that goes into being a successful angler. The release of a beautiful and unpredictable game fish involves almost every skill and talent a person may have. These brief successful ventures have stimulated me to learn as much as I can. Fishing is a lifelong sport that will last me to my dying day. I'm glad Rose took me under her wing when I was seven.

202 South Montana St.
Butte, Montana 59701
PH: 406-723-6526
FX: 406-782-9712

George Anderson

Age: 49

Camera-Film: Nikon, EPP 100, Fuji 100

Started fly fishing at age 12

Over the years I've written a lot about trout fishing in the magazines but I'll confess that saltwater fly fishing has become my first love. I got into saltwater fishing as a boy of 12, fishing with my dad while on winter vacations in Naples, Florida, where we caught small tarpon, snook, jacks and anything else we could find in the back country of the Ten Thousand Islands. Twenty years later I got back into saltwater fly fishing after an exciting tarpon trip to Costa Rica, and I've loved every minute of it since.

Learning everything I could about fly fishing for fish like bonefish, permit, and tarpon was (and still is) a real challenge. Lately I've had fun tackling blue water species like marlin, sailfish, and tuna as well. Best of all, I've found a wonderful new way to extend my fly fishing season throughout the year.

In all of my fishing (and hunting) exploits, I've dragged cameras along with me and have taken lots of photos. At first I used these slides to make up shows for family and friends, then later for fly fishing clubs, national fly fishing shows, and to accompany articles on fly fishing I've written for various fly fishing magazines. I now live in Livingston, Montana, and own The Yellowstone Angler-a full service fly fishing store.

Box 660
Livingston, Montana 59047
PH: 406-222-7130

Pierre Affre

Age: 43

Camera-Film: Nikon, Fuji Velvia

Started fly fishing at age 14

Pierre Affre is a former veterinary surgeon who says he "had to turn to fishing journalism and fish photography after killing nearly all the dogs, cats, and parroqueets in the Latin Quarter district of Paris" where he had a small veterinary practice. Though his veterinary thesis at the Sorbonne was on Atlantic salmon, except for a few goldfish nobody ever brought fish—his true specialty—to his clinic. So to keep his "specialty" up-to-date he had to travel frequently from the rivers of the Pyrenees to Norway, through Scotland, Ireland, and the Faroe Islands, and from Ungava Bay to the Kola Peninsula, through Labrador, Greenland, and Iceland. He theorizes that perhaps because he killed so many domestic animals he is now an ardent advocate of "no-kill" for wild salmonids. Pierre lives in Paris for the small portion of the year when he is not fishing for salmon, tarpon, or other great fresh and saltwater game fish.

59 Rue Dauphine
75006 Paris, France
PH: 1-432-60504
FX: 1-432-96553

Karl "Andy" Anderson

Age: 32

Camera-Film: Canon, Fuji Velvia

Started fly fishing at age 21

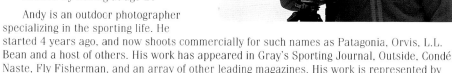

Andy is an outdoor photographer specializing in the sporting life. He started 4 years ago, and now shoots commercially for such names as Patagonia, Orvis, L.L. Bean and a host of others. His work has appeared in Gray's Sporting Journal, Outside, Condé Naste, Fly Fisherman, and an array of other leading magazines. His work is represented by several leading stock agencies and is marketed worldwide.

When shooting I try to extract the graphic and human elements and combine the two to make the image complete. I'm always trying new angles and lighting techniques to make a better image.

I shoot all sporting lifestyles from fly fishing, river rafting, bird hunting, to falconry. I feel variety in shooting subjects opens your perspective for more fresh ideas.

Saltwater is a photographer's dream. The light on the flats lasts so much longer that shooting time is increased. The colors are another thing that is my favorite. Mid-day light turns the bottom of a flat to very surreal hues. The variety of results can be endless with these types of things working in your favor.

The types of film that I shoot are mainly Fujichrome 50, Velvia for early morning and late afternoon, and Kodachrome. The cameras I use are Canon F-1 and L series lenses. I prefer the manual focus over autofocus because of the creative aspect.

When not chasing great light and images Andy can be found involved in all types of outdoor sports. He immensely enjoys the sport of wind surfing. Andy is married and has 3 children.

8115 N. Maple
Fairchild AFB
Washington 99011
PH: 509-244-5980

Joel Arrington

Age: 53

Camera-Film: Nikon, Fuji

Started fly fishing at age 30

After graduation from Duke University, Joel Arrington worked in North Carolina state government for over 20 years. In retirement, he engaged full-time in a free-lance writing and photography career he had begun years before.

A fly fisherman for over 25 years, Arrington has fished from Belize to Australia, but most of his experience has been in the ocean and sound waters around North Carolina's Outer Banks for red drum, giant bluefish and dolphin.

Arrington provides stock photos of fishing, hunting, and nature subjects to outdoor periodicals, agencies, and book publishers.

176 Roanoke Trail
Manteo, North Carolina 27954
PH: 919-473-3203

R.Valentine Atkinson

Age: 43

Camera-Film: Nikon, Leica, Fuji Velvia

Started fly fishing at age 5

R. Valentine Atkinson lives in San Francisco and is an internationally recognized travel & leisure photographer specializing in angling and shooting sports world wide. His work appears in *Esquire, Field & Stream, New York Times, VSD, Geo, Newsweek, Gray's Sporting Journal*, etc. Limited edition fine art prints are available.

"My life changed in 1985 when I became the staff photographer for Frontiers International Travel. I thought I had seen and done it all after 20 years in the business, then one day Susie Fitzgerald called and offered me my first assignment to Christmas Island. What an amazing opportunity and challenge it turned out to be. My senses were opened to a whole new dimension—saltwater fly fishing and photography.

Christmas Island had endless coral flats extending as far as the eye could see, terminated by billowy banks of cumulus clouds. Big, hungry, strong, fish that stripped out all of my backing, colorful, unusual, birds-some of which you could hold in your hands-hovered nearby. Small black tip sharks and pufferfish scurried off the flats in front of me. Every minute some new and unusual thing was happening. What a wonderful delight to one's senses. Over the years I've been to many new destinations and I can honestly say that almost nothing gets me so excited as the prospect of saltwater fly fishing. Just do it!

1263 6th Ave.
San Francisco, California 94122
PH: 415-731-4385
FX: 415-731-7712

Jose Azel

Age: Born Aug. 18, 1953

Camera-Film: Canon EOS, Leica M6, Kodak and Fuji transparency Film

Started fly fishing at age 10

Jose Azel attended Cornell University, where he began shooting pictures as a hobby. After completing his masters in journalism at the University of Missouri, he was hired as a staff photographer at the *Miami Herald*. In 1983, he joined Contact Press Images. The subjects he has covered vary greatly from sports to politics. A taste for adventure, an interest in environmental problems and a keen curiosity have led him to locations as diverse as the icy waters of Antarctica and Alaska, the game reserves of Kenya, and the jungles of Borneo. In 1993 he founded the photo agency AURORA with Bob Caputo. Azel continues to work for *National Geographic*, and also regularly shoots for *Smithsonian, Life, National Geographic Publications, Time Inc. Publications, Connoisseur*, The *London Sunday Times* magazine and *Geo* magazine.

"I think I'm a photographer because of my curiosity. I have a very wide range of interests, and being a photographer allows me to explore and expand those interests. I received

my first camera as a high school graduation present, and that's what really got me started—the whole process of satisfying my curiosity about that camera, how it worked and how clicking the shutter produced a certain kind of picture on the other end."

"When I was a little kid in the wilds of southern New Jersey, there was an old men's home not far from my house, and the old men used to fish with a stick and string and a bit of cork. One day one of the old men asked me if I'd like to try it, and gave me my own stick and string and cork. We dug up some worms, and he told me to out my line in a certain spot-'the fish like to hang out there'. I can still see my cork floating out on the eddy from the drainage pipe. And sure enough, a couple of minutes later I had my first fish! It was a perch. I hopped on my bike and pedaled home and filled up the bathtub for that perch to live in. It was completely ungrateful though—it died that night. My grandmother probably ate it–she loved fish.

RR #1 Box 924
East Stoneham, Maine 04231
PH: 207-925-3535

Bill Barnes

Age: 55

Camera-Film: Nikon, K64, Ektachrome

Started fly fishing at age 10

Bill has been an outdoor enthusiast since his childhood. He's a man of many talents. He was a physical education teacher in south Florida and was an outdoor editor for the Miami Daily News. He has traveled all over the world searching for great fishing and bird hunting. In the early 70's he began running Casa Mar on the Rio Colorado in Costa Rica.

16955 Southwest 286th St.
Homestead, Florida 33030
PH: 305-248-1246

Dan Blanton

Age: 49

Camera-Film: Nikon, Kodachrome 64

Started fly fishing at age 11

"I've always loved the outdoors, fishing almost every day before and after school as a child. 'Fanatical' best described me then. In 1954, using an old Japanese bamboo rod, I took my first fish on a fly at age 11. I pursued trout in the eastern Sierras until age 15. In 1958, I took my first striped bass on a fly, becoming hopelessly hooked on saltwater fly rodding. Since my early twenties, I've fly fished and photographed extensively throughout Central America, South America, and the Florida Keys. I've been a professional outdoor writer/photographer since 1975, with my work appearing in all of the leading fly fishing periodicals."

6130 Springer Way
San Jose, California 95123
PH: 408-365-2261

Jeffrey Cardenas

Age: 37

Camera-Film: Nikon, Fuji film

Started fly fishing at age 22

Jeffrey Cardenas lives in Key West and has been a flats guide with superb credentials. He was voted guide of the year by *Fly Rod & Reel* Magazine. He is an accomplished writer and photographer. He is the owner of The Saltwater Angler, Inc., a direct marketing company selling high end gear to serious saltwater fly fishermen.

He was nominated for the Pulitzer Prize for International Reporting in 1981 for work documenting the Cuban exodus from Mariel Harbor. He was a contract freelance photographer for the Associated Press, UPI, the *New York Times*, *Outside* magazine, and *Sports Illustrated*.

In 1984, he was awarded a fine art grant by the State of Florida to photograph underwater landscapes of the Florida Keys. His experience on the water includes 2500 days of documented sea service including three transatlantic crossings by sailboat.

Currently, Jeffrey is a monthly columnist and seminar leader for the top trade journal of fly fishing merchandising, *Fly Tackle Dealer*. He also writes a monthly column for *Fly Rod & Reel*, titled "Fly Fishing Success."

"One of my favorite writers has a wonderful expression. He says, 'If you are going to write abut fishing, don't.' The best writing about fishing, he explains, is not about the fishing at all. It is instead about the allure that brings us to the bright places where fish live. For me, fly fishing on the flats has very little to do with actually catching fish. In fact, catching the fish is often an anticlimax to the event rather than a culmination of the effort. I fish, and I photograph fish, because it is an opportunity for me to draw close to a truly wild thing. It is an opportunity to view first hand the life and times of creatures outside our element. We see the courtship of tarpon breaking out of daisy chains to travel as a pair. We feel the exuberance of a tailing bonefish when it finds a crab in shallow water. We witness the predatory drama of a blacktip shark chasing down and killing free swimming barracuda. Fishing is not about conquest and capture. It is about the love of a place and our bond with another species."

1218 Petronia St.
Key West, Florida 33040
PH: 800-223-1629

Hanson Carroll

Age: 64

Camera-Film: Canon, Fuji

Started fly fishing at age 41

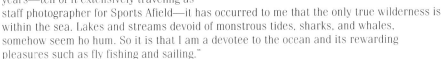

"Having been a photographer for 35 years—ten of it extensively traveling as staff photographer for Sports Afield—it has occurred to me that the only true wilderness is within the sea. Lakes and streams devoid of monstrous tides, sharks, and whales, somehow seem ho hum. So it is that I am a devotee to the ocean and its rewarding pleasures such as fly fishing and sailing."

"Recently, the joys of fly fishing were confirmed by a successful outing in the Florida Keys, my second home. As I was fly casting for tarpon near Indian Key in crystal smooth clear water, the VHF radio reported that 28 miles offshore, fishing boats in a tournament, with 112 baited lines in the water had produced nothing in the first hour. My first hour produced a 45 minute battle with a 75 pound tarpon fought on light tackle from my diminutive flats skiff, "Flats Rat". The contrast between the two types of fishing was incredibly clear. When it is good it is orgasmic but.....we all agree we catch less."

Winter: 223 Plantation Blvd   Summer: 11 New Boston Rd. Box 405B
          Islamorada, Florida 33036   Norwich, Vermont 05055
          PH: 305-852-9932   PH, FX: 802-649-1094

Trey Combs

Age: 53

Camera-Film: Nikon, Fuji

Started fly fishing at 16

Trey Combs has lived in Port Townsend, Washington for 25 years. An avid fly fisher for all game fish, he is best known for his articles and books on steelhead. Critics have called his most recent book, *Steelhead Fly Fishing*, Lyons & Burford, 1991, a classic on the subject. Saltwater fly fishing has taken him all over the world, including both coasts of South America and Africa. His fly fishing for billfish schools in Costa Rica and Mexico, his position as Contributing Editor of *Fly Fisherman Magazine*, his work in video productions , and on a new fly fishing book keep him on the road and fishing 200 days a year.

201 Victoria Loop
Port Townsend, Washington 98368
PH: 206-385-2530

Nick Curcione

Age: 50

Camera-Film: Nikon F-3, K64

Started fly fishing at age 27

In addition to his career as professor of sociology at Loyola Marymount University in Los Angeles, Nick is an outdoor writer/photographer/ lecturer and instructor with more than 30 years of angling experience. He has earned the reputation as an expert fly fisherman and is considered to be one of the pioneers of fly fishing the surf both in Southern California and Mexican waters.

His fishing travels have taken him to both coasts, Alaska, the Florida Keys, the Caribbean, Mexico, Central and South America. Nick has served as associate editor for California Angler and fly fishing editor for *Pacific Fisherman*. In addition, he regularly contributes to both local and national publications.

Recently he has signed on as a saltwater fly fishing consultant with Orvis and is currently writing Orvis's new *Saltwater Fly Fishing Handbook*.

"As a kid, my fishing experiences were primarily confined to summer outings on Long Island Sound. This is where my free spirited, jazz musician uncle introduced me to the fine art of fishing with a hand line. It was primitive, but it was fun. Years later when I started catching fish on fly gear, I realized that I was enjoying many of those same sensations I experienced with the simpler tackle. After all, fly fishing essentially involves using a hand line that you cast with a rod. Manipulating the line with your fingers, the dynamics of the strike and the fish's every movement is telegraphed directly to your sense of touch—a feeling that never ceases to spark my emotional circuits."

2021 Pullman Lane A
Redondo Beach, California 90278
PH: 310-376-9971

Gil Drake

Age: 52

Camera-Film: Pentax, Nikon, K64

Started fly Fishing at age 22

I was born and raised in Palm Beach. After attending the University of Miami, I went to work at my father's bonefish lodge at the east end of Grand Bahama, Deep Water Cay. There I guided parties for everything from bonefish to blue marlin. I also wrote articles and had photographs in *Field & Stream, Salt Water Sportsman, Sports Illustrated,* and *McClane's Fishing Encyclopedia.*

I began fishing as a child. My father taught me to use revolving spool reels and introduced me to tarpon, snook, and sailfish before I was 10 years of age. I learned to cast a fly while attending the University and spent more time chasing snook on the Tamiami canal than I ever did hitting the books. I did take a photography course which I really enjoyed and proved beneficial later on.

Besides fishing, skin-diving and hunting were my other major pursuits and, of course, photography fit right in. After 10 years of guiding in the Bahamas I moved to Key West where I could guide for tarpon and permit. During the summers and fall I fished and hunted out west.

Recently, I have been guiding year round in Florida—winter and early summer in Key West for tarpon, permit, and bonefish. From late summer through early winter I guide in the 10,000 Islands area of Everglades National Park for snook, redfish, and tarpon.

I have been fortunate enough to spend a lifetime of fishing and hunting and have done so in most of the United States, Canada, Iceland, Alaska, the Bahamas, Mexico, Costa Rica, Venezuela, and Ecuador.

Most of my photography has involved fish or wildlife. For this reason and because I rarely set up a shot, I keep my gear to a minimum. A couple of 35mm Pentaxes with lenses between 28mm and 200mm meet my topside needs. Under water a Nikonos with a 35mm lenses does the trick.

Basically I'm a hunter. I love working out the habits of fish and game. The chase and the final stalk are my raison d'etre. The kill is no longer important. In fact, as I have matured, the kill has become abhorrent. This has posed some serious dilemmas. Using a camera afield has posed a partial solution to a successful hunt without the necessity of a dead carcass. A friend once asked me, "Do you know what I mean by the essence of the moment?" I did. That second the quarry has committed itself. The fly balanced on a tarpon's snoot before he takes. The glint of sun on horn in a dense stand of lodgepole when a big bull takes up the challenge of your bugle. Mallards' wings set over decoys. For me the kill now ruins those beautiful moments, but a camera can give me a chance to preserve them.

2 Bougainvillea
Key West, Florida 33040
PH: 305-296-4905

Chico Fernandez

Age: 53

Camera-Film: Nikon, Leica rangefinder, Fuji 50

Started fly fishing at age 15

Chico lives in Miami where he photographs, writes, instructs and serves as a tackle consultant. Chico first learned fly casting as a boy while living in Cuba. Chico is a superb fly caster and is an instructor in the Florida Keys Fly Fishing school. He is quite famous for his innovative fly tying, and the "Bonefish Special," is his creation. He has many fly fishing world records to his credit. He is a staff writer for *Florida Sportsman.* Chico is a true sportsman who has an avid interest in the ecosystem of the Everglades and the Florida Keys.

11450 S.W. 98th St.
Miami, Florida 33176
PH: 305-596-4481

Christine Fong

Age: 50

Camera-Film: Canon, Fuji 50, K64

Started fly fishing at age 32

Christine studied fine arts at California College of Arts and Crafts in Oakland, CA. She has been photographing since the mid seventies, focusing primarily on fishing and outdoor related subjects. Her photographs have been published in all the leading outdoor periodicals including *Outdoor Life, Field and Stream, Sports Afield, Gray's Sporting Journal, Fly Fisherman, Fishing World, Fly Fishing* and others. She has traveled extensively throughout the United States, the Bahamas, throughout Central and South America, and New Zealand.

She has a passion for photographing insects, butterflies, birds, animals, and flora. She took up fly fishing at about the same time as photography and finds the two pursuits compatible and challenging.

Christine likes meeting people in different countries and unfamiliar places and to learn about their cultures and histories. She is interested in archaeology and treasures a few arrowheads found on fishing and photographic excursions in the west and southwest.

She fell in love with the tropics and bonefishing after catching her first bonefish on a fly on the flats of Guanaja off Honduras in 1980. The saltwater flats are special places for her. She finds the rise and fall of the tides and how these factors affect the behavior of bonefish fascinating. It is a constant challenge trying to figure out what they will do and how to coax them to bite. When not fishing she loves to gather a shell and hold it up to her ear to hear the sound of the sea.

Box 31282
San Francisco, California 94131
PH: 415-586-7668

Rod Harrison

Age: 48

Camera-Film: Nikon, Kodachrome, Velvia

Started fly fishing at age 23

Rod is a world famous guide located in Australia who takes specialty trips throughout Australia and New Guinea. He is an avid fly fisher and has a black marlin on a fly to his credit. He specializes also in shallow water trips and is a superb barramundi guide. He invented a fly called "The Pink Thing," the best all around barra fly.

Box 42
Briebie Island 4507
Australia
PH: 011-617-4080-334

Ed Jaworowski

Age: 50

Camera-Film: Nikon, Fuji Velvia

Started fly fishing at age 12

Ed is an Assistant Professor and Chairman of the Department of Classical Studies at Villanova University. He has written and photographed extensively and authored one book "The Cast, A Pictorial Guide to Fly Casting." He is an instructor and lecturer at "SAGE" Casting and Fishing Schools. He's a tackle consultant and field tester for tackle manufacturers including Sage, Simms, Umpqua, Scientific Anglers and Partridge. He was a former tournament surf caster.

"I relish the endless learning opportunities fly fishing presents. Each new species I target compels me to learn about the fish, its habits, habitats, foods; then the tackle, flies and techniques needed to take them, not to mention travel opportunities just to get to them. Nothing can duplicate the take of that bluefish, striper or snook that happened as a result of planning, anticipation, or mastery of some little subtle technique. The excitement of learning, studying, discovering–that's the magic of saltwater fly fishing for me."

505 Pickering Station Drive
Chester Springs, Pennsylvania 19425
PH: 215-594-8294

Brian O'Keefe

Age: 38

Camera-Film: Canon, Fuji

Started fly fishing at age 8

Brian is a freelance photographer specializing in fishing and athletic outdoor subjects. He reps for Scott Rods, Scientific Angler, Lamson Reels, Umpqua Feather Merchants and Barbour Clothing.

"I have always been fascinated by maps. I have a closet full of charts that show in great detail the world's most remote islands, shorelines, estuaries, river mouths and oceans. The world is 65% water and it only depresses me to think of all the great fishing that is not available only because of the life span of an average human being. So, live long, cast far, and leave a fished out corpse."

"Some photos in this book are available in large, 30 by 40 inch or larger super high quality color expansions. Write me or call!"

Box 5844
Bend, Oregon 97708
PH: 503-389-3474

Bob McNally

Age: 42

Camera-Film: Canon, Kodachrome 64, Fuji 100

Started fly fishing at age 4

Bob McNally is a full-time professional outdoor writer/photographer/broadcaster living near Jacksonville, Florida.

After graduating from the University of Wisconsin with degrees in journalism and English, Bob became outdoor editor of part of the *Chicago Tribune*, where his well-known fly fishing father Tom was outdoor editor for over 30 years. He lives on the St. Johns River, and 8 miles from the saltwater Intracoastal Waterway, 12 miles from the Atlantic Ocean, and within 50 miles of 6 major ocean inlets–all of which provide a wealth of fly fishing opportunities.

Bob has written nearly 2,000 feature magazine articles for every important outdoor publication in the United States. He is the author of 10 outdoor books and is on the writing staffs of *Southern Outdoors, Southern Saltwater, Florida Sportsman* and *Fishing Facts* Magazines. He currently is on the *Outdoor Life Magazine* fishing seminar staff. He is also a frequent seminar speaker for Saltwater Sportsman Magazine.

"Saltwater fly fishing also started early for me, even though I grew up outside Chicago. Every winter we traveled to Florida and the Bahamas, and Dad knew all the prime places and top fishermen. I remember fly fishing with Joe Brooks, Al McClane, Charlie Waterman, Dan Bailey, dozens of guides and others, and the stories of fish and fishing are forever ingrained. For me not fly fishing, especially in saltwater, would be like not walking or not eating."

"Photography of fly fishing was instilled early, as I helped my father as a youngster with photos. It was the norm to stop fishing and start shooting photographs when the light was right, the angle correct, and we had fish to record. I see those old photos all the time as I search my files for pictures—photos of places and friends, of memories and feelings impossible to describe with words."

"I can't imagine a richer way of life—fly fishing and shooting photos of it, for over 30 years. My children are growing up in much the same way I did, only living closer to saltwater and its infinite varieties of fly fishing. I only hope they continue to pursue these endeavors with the same passion that has proven to be such a rewarding way of life for me."

1267 Fruit Grove Drive
Jacksonville, Florida 32259
PH: 904-287-0917

Tim O'Keefe

Age: 49

Camera-Film: Nikon, Fuji 50, 100

Started fly fishing at age 40

Tim is a full time writer and photographer.

"I am a voyeur of long-standing. I started watching fish with a mask and snorkel around the age of 6, and I began photographing them underwater when I was 15. I enjoy the angling side, too, and that's what led me to fly fishing. Unfortunately, it's impossible to simultaneously fish and photograph, so I remain mostly a looker, through my viewfinder. For me, that's the best of both worlds. I often get just as excited as the angler I'm photographing, and my recorded memories are always sharper."

307 Fox Squirrel Lane
Longwood, Florida 32779
PH: 407-788-3062

Tony Oswald

Age: 42

Camera-Film:
> Canon, Nikon, 4x5 Calumet, Velvia, EPL 400

Started fly fishing at age 21

Tony is a full time photographer who grew up in Bad Hofgastein, Austria.

"My first recollection of water and life within it occurred while lying motionless on my stomach. I was staring into a small stream watching trout hold in the current, inches from my face. I was five years old then. I've held that image in mind ever since. With the camera, I try to convey visually the sensation of that elemental childhood experience."

"Gravitating to saltwater was a natural evolution. I fancy all anglers must eventually go to sea - the source of life - as a consummation of the connectiveness fly fishing gives one with all waters. For me, 'the long rod' is the most sensitive instrument."

"I currently have 27,000 computer cross-referenced images in stock including work by other photographers. World-wide coverage includes images of sport fishing, travel, landscape, people, wildlife & conservation."

> 33855 La Plata Lane
> Pine, Colorado 80470
> PH: 303-838-2203
> FX: 303-838-7398

Joe Richard

Age: 40

Camera-Film: Nikon, Fuji 100

Started fly fishing at age 30

"Well. Yes. My fishing began when I stretched a tape measure in the waters of Biscayne Bay near South Miami, at the tender age of six. Didn't have a hook or proper line, and didn't catch a fish that day."

"Things have improved since then. Or my catch rate anyway. My specialty is winning kingfish tournaments, and kingfish is the subject of my first book."

"After eight years of editing and shooting photographs for the Coastal Conservation Association's saltwater *Tide* magazine, I've been around. Saltwater resources have declined rather drastically in my short lifetime, and fighting that trend now seems my life's work."

> P.O. Box 205
> Port O'Connor, Texas 77982
> PH: 512-983-2731

C. Boyd Pfeiffer

Age: 55

Camera-Film: Nikon, K64, K400, Tri X

Started fly fishing at age 13

C. Boyd Pfeiffer is an award winning outdoor journalist widely known for his expertise in fresh and saltwater fishing, tackle, and outdoor photography. He has fished actively since a youth and contributed to the outdoor press for the past 25 years. In doing so, he has written hundreds of articles for over 50 magazines, served as outdoor editor of The Washington Post, lectured frequently, written many outdoor books, contributed to many others, and served as a consultant to the fishing tackle industry. He has authored and co-authored ten books on fishing and outdoor photography, including the classic *Tackle Craft* and his more recently published works including the *Orvis Guide to Outdoor Photography*, *Tackle Care* and *The Compleat Surfcaster*. He has had columns in or served as a contributing writer to a number of publications including *Sports Afield*, *Outdoor Life*, *The Washington Times*, *Bassmaster*, *Bassin'*, and others.

> 14303 Robcaste Road
> Phoenix, Maryland 21131
> PH: 410-527-0717

Jack Samson

Age: 70

Camera-Film: Nikon, Ektachrome, Kodachrome

Started fly fishing at age 7

Jack Samson was raised in Santa Fe, N.M., where he first developed his love of hunting and fishing. A graduate of the University of New Mexico (Journalism), he served four years in the Army Air Corps where he flew 52 combat missions in B-24 Liberators for Gen. Claire Lee Chennault's Flying Tiger 14th Air Force in China.

He returned to the Far East in 1950 and covered the Korean War as a war correspondent for United Press. As an Associated Press staff writer following the Korean War he was awarded a Nieman Fellowship to Harvard. He wrote an outdoor column for the AP and later joined the staff of *Field & Stream* in New York as managing editor in 1970. He became Editor-In-Chief in 1972 and held that position until 1983—when he became Editor-At-Large. He wrote 16 books while with the magazine and when he retired in 1985 he went on the masthead of *Western Outdoors* as Editor-At-Large.

The same year he became salt water editor of *Fly Rod & Reel* and fly fishing editor of *Marlin* magazine. Concentrating on salt water fly fishing, he won the 1989 International Fly Fishing Tournament in Costa Rica and by 1992 was the first angler in the world to catch both Atlantic and Pacific sailfish and all five species of marlin on a fly. His latest book—his 19th—is *Salt Water Fly Fishing*.

He lives with his artist wife, Victoria, in Santa Fe, N.M.

> 222 West Lupita Road
> Santa Fe, New Mexico 87501
> PH: 505-988-7118

Dale Spartas

Age: 42

Camera-Film: Canon EOS, Fuji Velvia, 50, 100

Started fly fishing at age 10

Dale C. Spartas is a full time free-lance outdoor photographer born and raised in Connecticut. As a boy he read about Montana in Joe Brooks' column and decided Montana was where he wanted to live, finally realizing his dream in 1988 with his family.

Spartas has always had a vast love and appreciation of the outdoors and is involved with hunting, fishing and conservation efforts. He spends much time training and hunting Purdey and Rose, his two Brittany Spaniels and his black lab Chip.

Subjects generally included in Dale's photographs are sporting dogs, upland birds and waterfowl, various fish species, hunting and fishing situations as well as scenic shots. Published in most of the outdoor magazines, Dale has also been a part of several books, calendars and advertising programs as well as being contributing photographer for *Gray's Sporting Journal*.

"The most important and satisfying thing we can do in the outdoors is give something back to it."

> 1120 Nelson Road
> Bozeman, Montana 59715
> PH: 406-585-2244

Walt Stearns

Age: 33

Camera-Film: Nikon, K25, K64, EPP 100

Started fly fishing at age 7

Born in Honolulu, Hawaii in 1960, Walt Stearns has been photographing the marine environment since high school and writing for the past seven years. He graduated from Miami Dade College in 1984 with a degree in Fine Arts and focused a great deal of his earlier years on the biological sciences. He worked as a diver for the Miami Seaquarium from 1982 through 1986, participating in numerous research projects involving manatees, dolphins and sharks.

Walt's writing, photography, and artwork has appeared in such publications as *Salt Water Sportsman, Field and Stream, Sport Fishing, Discover, Diving, Ocean Realm, Scuba Times, Sea Frontiers, BBC Publications, Wildlife, Tide, Outdoor Photographer,* and various other nature magazines. He is the boating editor for *Fishing World Magazine* and regular contributor to Conservation Association, Cousteau Society, and International Oceanographic Foundation. He is also an assistant dive instructor for the Professional Association of Dive Instructors (PADI).

Walt's professional travels have taken him to various locations including Alaska, the Bahamas, Belize, British Virgin Islands, Cayman Islands, Columbia, Costa Rica, the Figi Islands, Honduras, Mexico, Papua New Guinea, Tahiti, Trinidad/Tobago, Turks and Caicos, and Venezuela.

> 9121 S.W. 103rd Avenue
> Miami, Florida 33176
> PH: 305-598-7756

155

Bob Stearns

Age: 57

Camera-Film: Nikon, K25, K64, Fuji 50, 100

Started fly fishing at age 18

"A deep love of the outdoors, especially fishing and hunting, made full-time indoor employment an impossibility for me. That's why I spent seven years in environmental research field work with the U. of Miami's School of Marine & Atmospheric Sciences, and why I eventually moved on (1972) to become a full-time magazine writer and contributing editor to Field & Stream, Saltwater Sportsman, and Boating (currently), as well as Outdoor Life, Sports Afield, Fishing World, Fly Fisherman, Fly Fishing Quarterly, and many others over the years. My 'work' has taken me to many of the world's best fresh and saltwater fishing spots."

> 9000 S.W. 103rd Avenue
> Miami, Florida 33176
> PH: 305-595-5863

David Stoecklein

Age: 43

Camera-Film: Nikon, Kodak Films

Started fly fishing at age 18

"I was born in Pittsburgh, Pennsylvania and spent my childhood fishing small streams, lakes and ponds in and around Pittsburgh. I started fly fishing in 1970 on a trip to California for summer skiing and have been an avid fly fisherman ever since. I've been a photographer since I left college in 1969."

"My brother, Walter, and I have built a ranch in Mackay, Idaho, that has a spring creek and a large, spring-fed lake. We have dedicated a large portion of our lives and financial resources to protecting and improving our fish and wildlife habitats, as well as contributing to other conservation organizations. We both enjoy this with our families and especially enjoy teaching our families about fishing and the environment".

"I am a professional advertising photographer. My work has been featured in many national and international magazines, as well as in ads for sporting goods companies, and outdoor clothing and equipment. I use Kodak film exclusively and Nikon camera equipment. My favorite lens is the Nikor 600 mm f4 and I have eight F3 camera bodies and one F4 body, as well as 15 other Nikon lenses."

> Box 856
> Ketchum, Idaho 83340
> PH: 208-726-5191

Sam Talarico

Age: 49

Camera-Film: Minolta, Nikon, Fuji

Started fly fishing at age 20

"I bought my first camera, 'a Minolta SRT 101', after getting home from Woodstock in 1969. During the days that followed that monumental concert I thought, my God, it would have been great to be able to capture all those fantastic images on film. I remember that was how I felt when *LIFE* magazine came out with their Woodstock edition. I still have that book. I am a self taught photographer with no formal training. My passion for travel and meeting people of different cultures in their environments gave me plenty of opportunities for great photos. My main interest is to capture the spirit, life, and soul in people during their everyday lives, especially children."

"I live in the mountains of southeastern Pennsylvania. My house, out buildings and wine cellar that I have built are in a very secluded spot and have provided me with the peace to reflect on life and to be creative. I run a specialty hardwood lumber business which grew out of doing fine woodworking. I have also been a wine maker 25 years and have won many national awards."

"My need to be on the edge and to see fish in primitive and unspoiled places has gotten me involved in exploratory fishing in some wild places and has produced many great photos. The combination of saltwater fly fishing and being a photographer has added infinite pleasure to every trip I've been on. There is never a moment's rest. I'm never without a camera . My eye never stops looking for that perfect shot, the perfect light, that great action shot, and of course a great fish. I'm always on edge until I see my processed film to see if those special images I remember shooting are captured the way my eye saw them. I use both Nikon and Minolta equipment, and always carry a Nikon Actiontouch, a water proof camera, everywhere I go. It has gotten shots I normally would have missed. In my early days I shot mostly print film, but since have changed to mostly Fujichrome and Velvia film. My most extensive and current stock files are of Australia and Papua New Guinea, and consist of fishing, scenery and local culture shots."

"The most important event in my evolution as a fly fisherman and photographer was when I met Lefty Kreh. He has taught me so much that I consider him my mentor. It has been a joy to know him."

Rd #3 Box 3268
Mohnton, Pennsylvania 19540
PH: 215-775-3145

Mike Wolverton

Age: 48

Camera-Film: Nikon, Velvia, K64

Started fly fishing at age 9

Mike Wolverton was born in Santa Ana, California.

He has been fly fishing since the early age of nine. His father was a native of Montana and when the family would return to Montana to visit relatives, time was always set aside for fishing. During the ensuing years, Mike began to sample waters in other western states.

In the mid-sixties, Mike moved to Idaho, involving himself in the family ranching business. However, he returned to California at every opportunity to fish in the saltwater.

His commitment to writing and photographing his sport has escalated his travels and has been responsible for his traveling to numerous "exotic" destinations such as the Bahamas, the Cayman Islands, Christmas Island, Mexico, Belize, Costa Rica, Honduras, Venezuela, and others. These treks have produced catches ranging from bluefish to bonefish and billfish to wahoo, plus a multitude of other species.

Mike has had numerous photographs and angling related articles published in magazines and related media such as *Fly Fisher*, *Fly Fishing*, *Fly Fisherman*, *Saltwater Fly Fishing*, International Sportsman's Exposition brochures, Frontiers Travel brochures, Turneffe Flats Lodge brochures, and Bristol Bay Lodge brochures, etc.

In addition, Mike co-edited the book *Fly Fishing Always*, and, annually co-edits his wife, Bobbi's, famous Angler's Calendar collection. He is currently saltwater editor for *Fly Fishing* Magazine and contributes a regular column to that magazine called, "The Saltwater Journal." He has just recently become a member of the Outdoor Writer's Association of America, a professional journalist organization whose members specialize in outdoor communications.

In addition, Mike is a consultant for Sage Rod Co., Streamline, Cortland Line Co., Umpqua Feather Merchants, and others. He also works in an advisory capacity for several fishing lodges and travel agencies. He currently serves as a senior advisor to the Federation of Fly Fishers.

4955 E. 2900 N.
Murtaugh, Idaho 83344
PH: 208-432-6611

Bobbi Wolverton

Age: None of your business

Camera-Film: Nikon, Fuji

Started fly fishing 20 years ago

Barbara Phelps (Bobbi) Wolverton has been taking fishing photographs for over twenty years, and as a culmination of her work, created the *ANGLER'S CALENDAR* in 1976. She has received national recognition for her photographs and has had her work displayed in catalogs, books, brochures, slideshows and magazines around the world. Bobbi co-edited *Fly Fishing Always* and because of her work, received the Arnold Gingrich Memorial Life Membership from the Federation of Fly Fishers.

4955 E. 2900 N.
Murtaugh, Idaho 83344
PH: 208-432-6625